HYDERA

TRAVEL GUIDE

2025

Honest travel advice, local insight, and practical wisdom for seeing the city with clarity, not chaos.

Alma M. Wade

TABLE OF CONTENTS

INTRODUCTION..7

A (Not-So-Boring) Brief History of Hyderabad..........9

Why Visit Hyderabad?.. 12

CHAPTER 1: FIRST THINGS FIRST — WHAT YOU REALLY NEED TO KNOW BEFORE YOU LAND...... 15

Do you need a visa? (And how to not overthink it). 15

Best times to visit: Weather, festivals & when to skip the crowds... 18

How many days is "just right" in Hyderabad?........ 20

Quick cultural cheat sheet (So you don't offend anyone)...22

Travel insurance, safety basics & common rookie mistakes...24

Realistic expectations vs. Instagram fantasy..........26

CHAPTER 2: PLANNING LIKE A PRO — FLIGHTS, STAY, MONEY & SIM CARDS.................................... 28

Booking flights the smart way (when, how, and where to land)..28

Where to stay (by vibe, budget, and location)........ 30

Wi-Fi, SIM cards & how to actually stay connected in 2025...32

Currency, ATMs, UPI, tipping and the whole money thing... 35

How much will it really cost you per day?.............37

CHAPTER 3: GETTING AROUND WITHOUT LOSING YOUR MIND.. 41

Auto rickshaws, cabs, metros, and yes, traffic........41

Google Maps vs. local reality.............................44

Public transport hacks & how not to get ripped off. 46

How women can navigate Hyderabad safely and confidently..48

Day trip logistics — getting out of the city and back in one piece...50

CHAPTER 4: TASTE HYDERABAD — WHAT TO EAT (AND WHAT NOT TO MISS)...................................53

Must-try dishes: Biryani (of course), but also what else?...53

Local food joints, hole-in-the-walls, and royal kitchens...54

Where vegetarians (and vegans) won't feel left out56

Food safety tips: How to eat well without hugging the toilet...57

Sweet tooth satisfaction: Irresistible desserts you'll crave later..58

CHAPTER 5: THE HEART OF HYDERABAD — HISTORY, HERITAGE & ICONIC SITES.................... 61

Charminar, Chowmahalla, and the Old City's royal pulse..61

Golkonda Fort: Echoes, tunnels, legends, and the views...63

Qutb Shahi tombs, Mecca Masjid & beyond..........64

Museums that don't feel boring............................65

Walking tours and why they beat tour buses every time..67

CHAPTER 6: CULTURE, RELIGION, AND DAILY Life — WHAT MAKES HYDERABAD FEEL LIKE HYDERABAD...69

Language, dress codes, and street etiquette......... 69

A Hindu-Muslim cultural blend you won't find anywhere else..........71

Religion & rituals: What to know when visiting mosques and temples..........72

Local celebrations, weddings, and what that loud street procession really is..........73

How to respectfully blend in (and when to just be a curious tourist)..........74

CHAPTER 7: SHOPPING & MARKETS — WHAT TO BUY AND WHERE TO BARGAIN..........76

Laad Bazaar, pearls, perfumes, bangles and bling 76

Modern malls vs. old markets — where the magic really is..........78

What's worth your money (and what's just tourist bait)..........79

Bargaining tips that won't make you feel awkward. 81

How to ship stuff home if your suitcase gives up....82

CHAPTER 8: OFFBEAT HYDERABAD — HIDDEN GEMS YOU'D NEVER FIND ON GOOGLE..........85

Stepwells, secret cafés, lakeside spots and rooftop views..........85

The art scene, indie bookstores, and quiet escapes.. 86

Places even locals forget about..........87

Underrated temples, old havelis, and colonial corners..........88

Day trips that don't feel touristy..........90

CHAPTER 9: MODERN HYDERABAD — TECH CITY VIBES AND WHAT'S CHANGED..........92

Hitech City, start-up buzz, and the new Hyderabad92

Where young locals hang out — cafés, clubs, and

creative spaces..93

Health & wellness: Gyms, yoga, and where to detox after food marathons...94

Digital nomad friendly? (Spoiler: Yes — if you know where to go)..95

Hyderabad after dark — is it safe, fun, or both?.....96

CHAPTER 10: SAMPLE ITINERARIES & TRAVEL SMARTS.. 98

1-Day, 3-Day, and 5-Day itineraries that don't feel rushed..98

What to do if it rains (or your plan goes sideways)..... 100

How to slow down and travel well........................101

What locals wish tourists knew............................ 102

Final packing checklist (with zero fluff)................. 103

Parting tips to leave with memories, not regrets...105

INTRODUCTION

So... why Hyderabad?

I'll be honest with you — when people think about India, they usually picture the Taj Mahal, Rajasthan's deserts, maybe Kerala's backwaters, or the chaos of Delhi. Hyderabad? It's like the best-kept secret that somehow slipped through the cracks of every cookie-cutter travel list. And that's exactly why you need to go.

This guide was written for *you*. Whether you're planning your very first trip to India or you've already ticked off a few cities and want something richer, deeper, spicier (literally and figuratively) — Hyderabad is going to surprise you in the best way possible.

It's not just another city. It's a *collision of centuries*. One minute you're wandering through 16th-century Mughal palaces, and the next, you're sipping pour-over coffee in a sleek café beside coders and creatives in Hitech City. It's old and new, loud and soulful, gritty and glamorous — all at once. And trust me, it works.

But here's the thing: Hyderabad doesn't hand itself to you on a silver platter. It doesn't scream for your attention like some other cities. Instead, it rewards the curious. The ones who look a little closer. The ones who get a little lost in the bylanes behind Charminar or try a random dish they can't pronounce from a cart with no signboard.

That's where this book comes in.

This isn't some recycled list of "Top 10 Things to Do." No. This is your go-to, real-talk, no-fluff guide to navigating Hyderabad *your way*. We'll talk street food that slaps, transport that may test your patience (but I've got hacks), locals who will surprise you with warmth, neighborhoods that don't make it to Pinterest, and hidden gems that even TripAdvisor hasn't caught onto yet.

We'll keep it honest. What's worth your time? What's overhyped? What can you skip? What'll make you stay out an extra night even though you promised yourself you'd sleep early?

I've wandered those chaotic bazaars, climbed those sun-baked fort walls, and — yes — had one too many plates of biryani in search of *the one*. And now I'm putting everything I wish someone had told me into your hands.

So, if you're ready to ditch the generic tours and experience Hyderabad like a curious, open-hearted traveler—not a checklist-chasing tourist—you're in the right place.

Let's explore the City of Pearls together.
Let's do this right.

A (Not-So-Boring) Brief History of Hyderabad

Let's rewind the clock—way back to **1591**. Picture this: a hilltop, a river nearby, and a young ruler named **Muhammad Quli Qutb Shah**, who looks out over the land and decides, "Yup, this is it. This is where we build something big."

And so, Hyderabad was born.

Now, this wasn't just a random city plopped on a map. Quli Qutb Shah wasn't your average sultan. He was a poet, a dreamer, and someone who actually believed a city could be built on principles of beauty, order, and inclusivity. Legend has it he named it after **Bhagyamati**, a woman he loved, who later took the name **Hyder Mahal**—giving the city its name: **Hyderabad**, the "City of Hyder."

Romantic, right?

But it wasn't just hearts and poetry. Hyderabad quickly grew into one of the most cosmopolitan, culturally rich cities in the region. Under the Qutb Shahi dynasty, it became a hub for **Persian art**, **Indo-Islamic architecture**, and some seriously next-level planning—wide roads, grand arches, and oh, that now-iconic **Charminar** smack in the middle of it all.

Then came the **Mughals**. As empires do, they swept in by the late 1600s, led by Emperor **Aurangzeb**, and the Qutb Shahi dynasty faded out. But Hyderabad didn't lose its spark—it just shifted gears.

Enter the **Nizams**.

For over two centuries, the Nizams ruled Hyderabad as one of the richest princely states under the British Raj. And when I say rich, I mean **absurdly rich**. At one point, the **7th Nizam, Mir Osman Ali Khan**, was listed as *the* richest man in the world. The guy reportedly had diamonds the size of potatoes just... lying around.

Under the Nizams, Hyderabad saw a golden age of development—railways, education, hospitals, even a high-tech water supply system (yes, before most places even had pipes). But it wasn't just the bling and buildings; it was a mix of **Urdu poetry**, **Telugu theatre**, **Marathi literature**, and a culture that blended Hindu, Muslim, and even British influences into something uniquely Hyderabadi.

Then came **1948**, a crucial turning point. After India gained independence in 1947, the Nizam wasn't exactly eager to join the new country. Long story short: the Indian government said "enough waiting," rolled in troops (in what they called **Operation Polo**), and Hyderabad officially became part of India.

Fast forward to today, and you'll see those layers still alive. The old city echoes the Qutb Shahis. The palaces and pearls whisper of the Nizams. And the glass towers in **Hitech City** shout about the future. It's all here—stacked together in one city that never quite forgot where it came from, even as it races ahead.

So yeah, Hyderabad's not just "a place."
It's a 400-year-old love story, empire drama, and tech fairy tale rolled into one.

Cool, right?

Why Visit Hyderabad?

So you're on the fence. Hyderabad's not the first city that pops into your head when you think "bucket list," right? I get it. It doesn't have the Taj Mahal. It's not splashed across Instagram with colorful saris in desert backdrops. It doesn't shout.

But *that's exactly the point.*

Hyderabad doesn't need to show off. It just is. And once you're there, it grabs you in the quietest, most unexpected ways.

Here's the thing — if you're the kind of traveler who chases real flavor (I mean that literally *and* metaphorically), Hyderabad will reward you tenfold.

Food lovers, let's start with you. Ever heard people argue about where to find the *best biryani in India*? Spoiler: this is ground zero. But it's not just about the biryani (though yeah, you'll dream about it afterward). From spicy street-side snacks to centuries-old royal recipes, the food scene here is intense, addictive, and surprisingly affordable. You could spend a week eating your way through this city and never repeat a single dish.

History buffs? Welcome to paradise. This place has layers—like, onion levels of history. You've got 400-year-old mosques standing just a short ride away from sprawling tech campuses. One moment you're hearing the echo of footsteps through Golkonda Fort, the next you're sipping artisanal coffee in a startup lounge. It's surreal—in the best way.

Culture seekers, Hyderabad is where north meets south, where Urdu poetry blends with Telugu folk music, where Hindu festivals and Islamic traditions live side by side. And the best part? It doesn't feel staged or curated for tourists. It's just... real.

Now, if you're someone who loves **cities with soul**, not just surface, Hyderabad gives you that. It's messy in parts, yes. Traffic can test your patience. But then you turn a corner and stumble into a quiet shrine glowing under fairy lights. Or you meet a local who insists you try a dessert you've never heard of—*on them*. It's a place where ordinary moments suddenly feel meaningful.

And hey, **if you're a peace-seeker**, don't write it off just yet. There are calm lakes, quiet tombs, rooftop cafés, and parks where time slows down. You'll find your pace here, whatever it is.

So no, Hyderabad doesn't come at you with filters and fireworks. But if you're looking for a destination that feels *undiscovered but full of life, historic but buzzing with energy, chaotic yet strangely comforting* — then yeah, Hyderabad's absolutely worth the trip.

Just bring an open mind, a hungry stomach, and maybe a stretchy waistband.

CHAPTER 1: FIRST THINGS FIRST — WHAT YOU REALLY NEED TO KNOW BEFORE YOU LAND

Do you need a visa? (And how to not overthink it)

If you're not an Indian passport holder, then yes, you probably need a visa to visit Hyderabad—and honestly, it's not as scary as it sounds.

India's e-Visa system has made things a lot simpler over the past few years. Most travelers can now apply online through the official portal: https://indianvisaonline.gov.in. And **yes, that's the only site you should use**—don't fall for unofficial "helper" websites that charge extra fees or worse, ghost you after payment.

There are a few types of visas depending on why you're visiting. For tourists, you'll want the **e-Tourist Visa**. It's available in 30-day, 1-year, and 5-year versions. The 30-day visa is double entry (so you can leave and re-enter once), and the longer ones are multiple entry—handy if you're hopping around Asia.

The application itself is fairly straightforward. You'll need:

- A clear scanned copy of your passport (valid for at least 6 months)

- A recent passport-style photo

- A working email address

- A credit/debit card for payment

Processing time usually takes around **3–5 working days**, but don't cut it close. If you're on a tight schedule, *don't* book flights until your visa is approved—just in case. Delays can happen, especially around Indian holidays or big travel seasons.

Also worth knowing: upon arrival in India, your fingerprints and photo will be taken as part of the biometric process. It's quick, but don't be surprised. Some nationalities (like Pakistan, Afghanistan, and others) may face more paperwork or require a regular sticker visa from a consulate.

A few pro tips:

- Triple check your passport number and birthdate before submitting.

- Keep a printed copy of your e-Visa just in case your phone dies.

- Avoid applying through a public Wi-Fi connection—yes, people still do that.

If you're a **digital nomad**, long-term traveler, or on a multi-country trip, the 1-year or 5-year visa gives you flexibility. But remember: you can only stay up to **90 days per visit**, even with a longer visa.

Oh, and don't fall for the trap of overcomplicating it. Thousands of travelers use the e-Visa system every day—it's not perfect, but it works. Just breathe, read carefully, and give yourself a bit of buffer time. You'll be fine.

Best times to visit: Weather, festivals & when to skip the crowds

Hyderabad doesn't have snow or dramatic seasonal changes like some places, but that doesn't mean the timing doesn't matter. In fact, it matters *a lot*.

Let's break it down.

Summer (March to June): Let's be real—Hyderabad in summer can be brutal. We're talking highs around **40°C (104°F)**, with dry, draining heat. If you're heat-sensitive, this might not be your season. That said, flights and hotels tend to be cheaper, and indoor attractions like museums and palaces are still doable if you start your day early and pace yourself. Sunscreen, light cotton clothes, and staying hydrated aren't optional—they're survival tools.

Monsoon (July to September): The rain brings relief from the heat, but also, well... rain. And humidity. Expect sudden showers, wet streets, and delays in outdoor plans. But it's not all bad—there's a certain magic to Golkonda Fort or the Qutb Shahi Tombs with moody skies and fresh air. Just pack an umbrella or a good rain jacket and some waterproof shoes.

Winter (October to February): This is peak travel time for a reason. The weather's pleasant—mild mornings, sunny afternoons, and cool evenings around **15–28°C (59–82°F)**. It's ideal for sightseeing, walking around bazaars, and just being outdoors. Of course, it's also when prices go up and popular spots get crowded, especially during school breaks in December.

Now, **festivals**.

- **Bonalu (July/August)**: Unique to Telangana. Expect vibrant parades, loud drums, and lots of energy in the Old City.

- **Ramzan (changes each year, expect around March-April in 2025)**: The Old City becomes a sensory overload in the best way—bazaars lit up at night, special foods like Haleem, and prayer calls echoing through the air.

- **Diwali (usually October or November)**: Firecrackers, sweets, lights everywhere. Beautiful, but noisy and chaotic too. Book early.

If you're not into crowds but still want great weather, aim for **late February or early October**—the sweet spots when it's pleasant but not packed.

For families or older travelers, **November and February** are great bets. Not too hot, not too cold, and fewer school-holiday crowds. Solo travelers might enjoy the buzz of Ramzan evenings, while foodies should time their trip around major feasting festivals.

How many days is "just right" in Hyderabad?

There's no one-size-fits-all answer here, but let's be practical.

If you're a **sightseeing sprinter**, you could technically hit the highlights in **2 days**—Charminar, Golkonda Fort, the chowk bazaars, and a couple of great meals. It'll be fast and full, but doable if you're passing through or doing a stopover.

For a **well-paced, thorough visit**, plan for **4 to 5 days**. That gives you time to explore the Old City, spend an afternoon around Hitech City or the newer parts of town, visit the Qutb Shahi Tombs, maybe take a walk around Hussain Sagar Lake, and still have time for good food and spontaneous detours. You'll feel like you got to know the city.

If you're planning to **do side trips**—say to Ramoji Film City, or maybe take it slow with a digital nomad vibe—**7+ days** is great. You'll get downtime, flexibility, and a real rhythm of life.

Also keep in mind:

- **Traffic is real**. An attraction "just 5 km away" can still take 40 minutes.

- Staying in a central area like Banjara Hills or Abids can save you time.

- If you're flying in from far away, factor in **jet lag**. Hyderabad's rhythm isn't forgiving if you're sleep-deprived.

For families with young kids or older travelers, **3–4 days** with built-in rest time works well. You don't need to see *everything*. The city's vibe soaks in better when you slow down a little.

Quick cultural cheat sheet (So you don't offend anyone)

Hyderabad is one of India's more laid-back big cities, but it still helps to know the basics. Here's the friendly crash course.

Dress modestly, especially in the Old City or at religious places. You don't need to wear traditional Indian clothes, but covering shoulders and knees is respectful and practical. Light, loose fabrics are your best bet in the heat anyway.

Temples and mosques: Always take off your shoes. In some places, you may also be asked to cover your head. Women might not be allowed into certain sections of mosques—don't take it personally. Just follow posted signs or politely ask a local.

Public displays of affection are generally frowned upon, especially in older areas. Holding hands? Fine. Kissing? Save it for private.

Greetings vary. A simple "namaste" with a small bow is polite in most settings. In Muslim-majority parts of the city, you might hear "salaam" or "assalamu alaikum." You don't *have* to use them, but it's a nice touch.

Haggling is totally normal in local markets, but do it with a smile. It's not war, it's a game. Don't bargain aggressively over a few rupees—it just makes things awkward.

Body language tip: avoid pointing with your finger, especially at people. Use your whole hand or gesture subtly.

Solo female travelers are common here, especially in newer parts of town. Just dress modestly, be firm with overfriendly strangers, and trust your instincts. Local women are often incredibly helpful if you need advice.

Languages can be a mix. Telugu is the state language, but Urdu is widely spoken in the Old City, and most locals speak at least basic English. You'll get by fine, but learning a few words always helps:

- *"Anna"* or *"akka"* (brother/sister in Telugu): a polite way to call someone's attention.

- *"Shukriya"* (thank you in Urdu): nice to know if you're shopping in the Old City.

Hyderabadis are generally warm, helpful, and full of stories if you show a little respect and curiosity.

Travel insurance, safety basics & common rookie mistakes

Let's get this out of the way: **yes, you need travel insurance**. Not maybe. Not "if you have room in the budget." Just get it.

Medical care in India is advanced and affordable, but without insurance, you'll pay out of pocket. And stuff happens—Delhi belly, sprained ankles on old steps, missed flights, you name it. Companies like **SafetyWing**, **World Nomads**, and **Allianz** offer solid options. Look for:

- Emergency medical coverage

- Trip cancellations/delays

- Lost baggage

- Coverage for adventure activities if you're planning any

Hyderabad is safer than many other big cities, but it's still a city. Common sense goes a long way.

Stick to well-reviewed accommodations. Areas like **Banjara Hills**, **Jubilee Hills**, and **Hitech City** are safe and traveler-friendly. The Old City is amazing for exploring but stay alert—it gets crowded, and pickpocketing can happen.

Use **official cabs**, ride-sharing apps like **Ola or Uber**, and avoid unmarked taxis, especially at night. Women should avoid walking alone in poorly lit or isolated areas. If you're LGBTQ+, know that Hyderabad is relatively accepting in modern circles, but discretion is still wise in traditional neighborhoods.

Some rookie mistakes to avoid:

- **Drinking tap water** — just don't. Buy sealed bottles or use a purifier.

- **Booking attractions last-minute** — places like Ramoji Film City can sell out.

- **Assuming distances are short** — traffic here laughs at your optimism.

- **Trusting random "tour guides" at landmarks** — stick to verified sources.

Save these local emergency numbers:

- Police: 100

- Ambulance: 108

- Tourist Helpline (India): 1800-11-1363

Trust your instincts, prep smart, and you'll be ahead of 90% of first-timers.

Realistic expectations vs. Instagram fantasy

Let's be honest: Instagram doesn't show you the full story. You'll see Charminar lit up against the sunset, plates of perfect biryani, colorful bangles gleaming in markets—and yeah, that stuff *is* real. But so are the power outages, construction noise, and scooter horns at 7 a.m.

Hyderabad is a living, breathing city. It's not airbrushed. It's loud, layered, messy, warm, confusing, funny, frustrating, and fascinating. You might sweat through your shirt while waiting in line for a palace. You might get stuck in traffic for 45 minutes just to move five kilometers. You might also meet a chai vendor who remembers your order the next day and waves like you're old friends.

This isn't a curated destination. It's an experience. And like any experience, it's better when you show up curious, not rigid.

The food may be spicier than you're used to. The buses may not run on time. Not everyone speaks fluent English. And yes, some popular spots are more hype than substance.

But here's what you get in return: an unmatched sense of place. Stories in every alley. Layers of culture you *feel*, not just read about. The kind of travel that stays with you long after you leave.

So manage your expectations, ditch the filters, and come with open eyes. If you do, Hyderabad will meet you halfway—and then some.

CHAPTER 2: PLANNING LIKE A PRO — FLIGHTS, STAY, MONEY & SIM CARDS

Booking flights the smart way (when, how, and where to land)

Getting to Hyderabad doesn't have to feel like solving a Rubik's cube blindfolded. If you know what to look for and when to book, your flight can be more of a bargain than a burden.

Hyderabad's main airport is **Rajiv Gandhi International Airport (HYD)**. It's modern, well-run, and about 30 kilometers (roughly an hour's drive, depending on traffic) from the city center. It handles both domestic and international flights, with major airlines like Emirates, Qatar Airways, British Airways, Singapore Airlines, Lufthansa, and Etihad flying in from major global hubs. For U.S. travelers, expect a layover—usually in Dubai, Doha, or Frankfurt.

If you're flying in from within India, airlines like IndiGo, Air India, Vistara, and SpiceJet offer frequent, affordable connections from cities like Delhi, Mumbai, Bangalore, and Chennai. Vistara tends to have a slightly more polished experience, while IndiGo is reliable and no-frills.

Google Flights is your best friend for scanning fares. Use **Skyscanner** for a broader sweep across budget airlines. **Hopper** is helpful for tracking when prices dip—especially useful if your travel dates are flexible. Start watching fares around **2–4 months in advance** for international trips and **3–6 weeks** for domestic.

Big money-saving tip: avoid flying during **Indian school holidays** (May–June and late December) and **festival seasons** like Diwali (Oct/Nov). If you must travel then, book as early as you can. Also, mid-week flights (Tuesdays and Wednesdays) are often cheaper than weekend departures.

When you land at HYD, things are mostly smooth—clean immigration counters, decent signage, free baggage carts. But don't expect it to be lightning fast. Visa-on-arrival queues (if applicable to your nationality) and document checks can stretch up to 45 minutes. Once you clear that, baggage claim and customs are usually quick unless you're arriving at peak hours.

Watch out for one common arrival scam: **unofficial taxi agents** inside the airport promising "discounted" rides. Politely decline. Use the **airport's prepaid taxi booth**, **Uber**, or **Ola** (India's local ride-share app) once you're outside the arrivals terminal.

If you're traveling with kids, know that **stroller access is decent**, but airport staff often offer help if you're struggling. **Wheelchair assistance** is available—just make sure to request it through your airline at least 48 hours before arrival.

Not sure if the airline is worth booking? Check reviews on **SeatGuru** or **Skytrax** before confirming. Better to avoid a 12-hour layover in a city you can't leave just to save $50.

Where to stay (by vibe, budget, and location)

Hyderabad is a sprawling city, and where you stay seriously shapes your experience. So don't just pick a place based on pretty photos. Pick a **neighborhood that fits your vibe**.

Banjara Hills: Think leafy lanes, boutiques, and upscale cafés. It's calm but central, great for first-timers who want comfort and convenience. You'll find everything from stylish boutique hotels to mid-range chains here. It's quiet at night and ideal for couples, families, or anyone who values sleep.

Jubilee Hills: Trendier and livelier than Banjara Hills. Known for swanky bars, designer stores, and celebrity homes. If you want nightlife and Instagrammable brunch spots, this is your zone. A bit pricier, but fun.

HITEC City: This is the tech and business district. Slick skyscrapers, global hotel chains, and co-working spaces. Great for digital nomads or business travelers. Less culture, more convenience.

Gachibowli: More spread out and a bit quieter, but also newer. Lots of corporate offices, expat-friendly housing, and modern apartment hotels. Ideal for long stays or travelers who don't mind being slightly farther from the old city action.

Old City: This is where Hyderabad's heart beats loudest. Charminar, bazaars, minarets, chaos. Budget travelers and backpackers will find cheap guesthouses here, but know it's noisy, crowded, and a bit rough around the edges. Not ideal if you're hoping for Wi-Fi that works every time or guaranteed hot water.

Mid-range and boutique hotels: Brands like **Treebo** and **FabHotels** are affordable and generally clean, but check recent reviews—quality can vary wildly by location. **Bloom Hotels** and **Lemon Tree** offer more consistent experiences. For something with character, look for small boutique stays in Banjara Hills or converted havelis near Falaknuma.

High-end options: The **Taj Falaknuma Palace** is a splurge—but an unforgettable one. Think royalty-level service and a view of the entire city. Other luxe picks include **ITC Kohenur**, **Park Hyatt**, and **Westin Hyderabad Mindspace**.

Solo female travelers might want to stick to Banjara Hills or HITEC City for peace of mind and access to essentials. Families will love apartment-style stays in Gachibowli, while romantic travelers should aim for a palace stay or charming boutique hotel.

Avoid super-remote listings unless you're staying long-term. And always read the fine print—some budget spots have "beautiful views" but no elevators or working AC.

Wi-Fi, SIM cards & how to actually stay connected in 2025

Getting connected in Hyderabad is straightforward—but there are still a few hoops to jump through if you want good service and a fair deal.

The big three telecom players are **Jio**, **Airtel**, and **Vi (Vodafone-Idea)**. All offer decent coverage in Hyderabad, but **Jio** is the front-runner for fast data and widespread 4G/5G access. **Airtel** is a close second with strong customer service. **Vi** is usually cheaper, but the signal can get patchy in older parts of the city.

You can buy a SIM card at the airport (there's an Airtel booth in the arrivals area), but it's often overpriced and occasionally understocked. If you're not in a rush, it's usually better to head into the city and visit an **official store**. Bring:

- Your **passport**

- A printed copy of your **visa/e-Visa**

- A **passport-sized photo** (some shops take one for you)

- A local address (your hotel works)

Activation time is usually within a few hours but can take up to 24 hours. Ask the staff to help set it up if you're unsure—most are used to assisting travelers.

Prepaid plans are cheap. You can get around **1.5GB/day + unlimited local calls** for 28 days at roughly **₹300–₹400**. Just make sure to ask for **international calling** and **data roaming** only if you actually need it.

If you have a phone that supports **eSIM**, check Jio's or Airtel's eSIM activation support. It can save you time, but the setup still requires a local ID or documentation, so it's not 100% frictionless.

Public Wi-Fi exists—in malls, cafés, hotels—but it's hit or miss. Speeds vary, and security is... questionable. Don't do banking or anything sensitive on shared networks unless you're using a **VPN**.

Apps like **MyJio**, **Airtel Thanks**, or **Vi app** help manage your plan, top up, and check data usage.

Digital nomads and remote workers should stick with Jio or Airtel, and consider staying in HITEC City or Banjara Hills where café Wi-Fi is more reliable and co-working spaces are abundant.

Avoid buying SIMs from shady kiosks or random vendors near train stations. These are notorious for overcharging or giving you pre-activated SIMs that could expire mid-trip.

Currency, ATMs, UPI, tipping and the whole money thing

India uses the **Indian Rupee (INR)**, and in 2025, the exchange rate hovers around **₹82–85 per USD**, depending on global swings. Always check a trusted source like **xe.com** before exchanging money.

Avoid converting large sums at the airport unless absolutely necessary—the rates are often poor, and service fees can be high. A better bet? Withdraw from an **ATM inside a bank branch** once you're in the city. It's safer, better rates, and you'll usually avoid double fees.

Most ATMs accept Visa and Mastercard, but not all are foreign-card friendly. **HDFC, ICICI,** and **Axis Bank** tend to be reliable for international cards. Expect a withdrawal fee of ₹200–₹500 depending on your home bank.

Now for the real MVP of Indian transactions: **UPI (Unified Payments Interface)**. It's a contactless payment system linked to mobile apps like **PhonePe, Google Pay,** and **Paytm**. You'll see even street vendors using QR codes. If you have an Indian SIM and bank account, you can set up UPI easily. Foreigners can now register using international debit/credit cards on certain apps—but it's still not seamless for all banks.

Until that's sorted, carry some **cash**. Small denominations are handy for local transport, snacks, temple donations, and tips.

As for **tipping**, it's appreciated but not always expected. Some basic guidelines:

- Restaurants: round up or leave **5–10%** unless service charge is already added.

- Hotel staff: ₹50–₹100 for bellboys or room service.

- Drivers: not mandatory, but rounding up or a ₹100 note for long rides is thoughtful.

- Tour guides: if you had a great experience, **₹200–₹300** is a nice gesture.

Beware of money scams. Don't change cash on the street. Always count your change. And if a price seems too high in a market, it probably is—negotiate respectfully.

A **money belt** or **hidden pouch** helps in busy areas like Charminar. Also, most modern travel wallets now have **RFID protection**, which is handy but not essential unless you're extra cautious.

How much will it really cost you per day?

Let's talk numbers. Here's what your daily spend might look like in Hyderabad in 2025, based on your travel style:

Budget backpacker (~₹1,500–2,000/day)

- Dorm bed or simple guesthouse: ₹500–800

- Street food or cheap thali meals: ₹300

- Local buses, metro, or shared autos: ₹100

- Entry fees: ₹100 200

- SIM/data: ₹20/day (avg)

- Extras (snacks, small souvenirs): ₹100–200

You'll get by comfortably if you keep it local. Just avoid over-relying on cabs or eating at touristy restaurants.

Mid-range explorer (~₹3,500–5,000/day)

- Mid-range hotel or nice Airbnb: ₹1,500–2,500

- Mix of casual dining + 1–2 nice meals: ₹800–1,200

- Ola/Uber + occasional autos: ₹300–500

- Entry tickets, museum passes: ₹300

- SIM/data + coffee stops: ₹100–200

- Shopping/souvenirs: ₹500

This is the sweet spot for most travelers—comfort, variety, and flexibility.

Comfort-first traveler (~₹8,000–12,000/day)

- Boutique or 4-star hotel: ₹4,000–7,000

- Fine dining, cocktails, room service: ₹1,500–2,500

- Private cabs or guided day tours: ₹800–1,200

- Entry fees + guided experiences: ₹500

- SIM/data + splurges: ₹200–500

- Shopping: ₹1,000+

You won't feel limited at this range—and can still avoid spending recklessly.

What's cheap: transport, food, local experiences, SIM cards
 What can sneak up: hotel taxes, entry tickets at palaces, tipping guides or drivers, boutique shopping

Don't cheap out on **bottled water**, verified transport, or hygiene. A few extra rupees go a long way in protecting your health and peace of mind.

If you're tracking your full trip cost, multiply the above by your days in town—and remember to pad your budget a little. Hyderabad is generous, but the temptations (and snacks) are real.

CHAPTER 3: GETTING AROUND WITHOUT LOSING YOUR MIND

Auto rickshaws, cabs, metros, and yes, traffic

Getting around Hyderabad is both an adventure and a lesson in patience. The city has options—some more charming than efficient—but if you know when and how to use each, it's pretty manageable.

Let's start with the most iconic ride: the **auto rickshaw**. You'll see these three-wheeled yellow-green machines zipping through traffic like they've got a secret shortcut to everywhere. They're fast, plentiful, and often cheaper than cabs for short trips. But here's the catch—**meters are more of a suggestion than a rule**. Some drivers will use them (especially near malls or metro stations), but many prefer to quote you a price upfront. Always ask for the meter. If they refuse and the price sounds too high, politely walk away. A fair rate for a 3–5 km ride might be ₹60–100 depending on traffic and time of day. Also, apps like **Ola Auto** and **Uber Auto** can help you avoid the back-and-forth bargaining.

Cabs (Ola and Uber) are your best bet for longer rides or airport transfers. They're air-conditioned, app-based, and more reliable than street taxis. Prices fluctuate with traffic and demand, but they're still very reasonable compared to Western cities. You can choose from standard, sedan, or SUV options. For solo travelers or couples, **Uber Moto** or **Rapido** (bike taxis) are faster and super cheap—just make sure you're okay with hopping on a stranger's two-wheeler and wearing a shared helmet.

Now, the **Hyderabad Metro**. It's clean, quick, and actually expanding. The **Red Line** (Miyapur–LB Nagar) and **Blue Line** (Nagole–Raidurg) are the most useful for travelers. They cover major areas like Ameerpet (interchange station), HITEC City (near tech offices), and MG Bus Station. It runs roughly from **6:30 a.m. to 10:30 p.m.**, with trains every 6–10 minutes.

Tourists should get a **stored-value smart card** (called the "TSavaari card") from the station counters—it saves time and avoids dealing with tokens every ride. Stations are clearly marked, and announcements are in English and Telugu. Security checks are standard at entrances, but nothing intimidating.

The **metro is especially great during rush hour** when roads are jammed. Speaking of which—let's talk **traffic**. Hyderabad traffic is legendary, and not in a good way. Between **8:30–10:30 a.m.** and **5:30–8:30 p.m.**, some parts of the city move at the pace of a tired cow. If you're traveling between major hubs like Jubilee Hills and Secunderabad, budget **double the expected time**. Always factor in buffer time before flights or train departures.

Comfort-wise, the metro wins. AC, reliable timing, and no dust storms. Autos are breezy but loud and bumpy. Cabs are comfy but stuck in traffic more often than not.

Tips for different travelers:

- **Families with strollers**: Metro stations have elevators, but not always near entrances. Carry a lightweight stroller if possible.

- **Seniors**: Stick to cabs or metro. Avoid autos unless the ride is very short.

- **Solo female travelers**: Ola and Uber have location sharing and SOS buttons. Metro has **women-only coaches**, usually at the front.

- **Couples**: Any transport works fine—autos are fun for short night rides.

- **Mobility concerns**: Metro is the easiest option. Some newer cabs are wheelchair-accessible, but they must be pre-booked.

Hyderabad's transport is far from perfect, but it's navigable once you know the quirks.

Google Maps vs. local reality

Google Maps in Hyderabad is kind of like that friend who means well but sometimes gets lost. It's incredibly helpful—until it isn't.

For **driving and cab rides**, Google Maps is generally accurate for routes and traffic estimates, especially in newer areas like HITEC City, Gachibowli, or Banjara Hills. But in the **Old City**, it can fall apart. Tiny lanes, ever-changing street directions, and unnamed alleys often confuse the system. You might be 50 meters from your destination and still not know where the entrance is.

For **walking**, it's hit or miss. Many sidewalks are either non-existent or used for parking. A 10-minute walk on the map might turn into a mini-obstacle course with honking traffic and sudden detours. That said, it's still useful for general direction—just don't trust it blindly.

For **public transport**, the app shows metro lines and estimated times decently, but doesn't always reflect train delays or station closures. Bus info is spotty. Timings might show up, but don't expect real-time accuracy.

Locals often double-check with **Zomato** when searching for restaurants, especially for updated location pins and reviews. You can also ask hotel staff to confirm an address or give you a landmark-based version ("Opposite KFC on Road No. 36")—Hyderabadis love giving directions this way.

Want a backup? Try **MapMyIndia** or **Here WeGo**—they're sometimes more detailed for older parts of the city. And always **download offline maps** before heading into less-connected areas. Having **landmark-based directions written down** (or saved as a photo on your phone) is smart.

Real talk: expect confusion in areas like **Charminar, Sultan Bazaar**, or any place with multiple shops of the same name. And neighborhoods with similar-sounding names—like

Malkajgiri and **Malkapuram**—are a classic trap for tired travelers.

Google Maps is a solid tool—but in Hyderabad, it's just that: a tool. Not gospel.

Public transport hacks & how not to get ripped off

Public transport in Hyderabad is a bit of a mixed bag. There's the **metro** (modern and efficient), **TSRTC buses** (cheap but a bit wild), and **MMTS trains** (old-school local trains, mostly for commuters).

Let's start with the **metro**—your best friend for long distances and avoiding peak-hour traffic. Fares are between ₹10 and ₹60 depending on the distance. Buy a **TSavaari smart card** at the station for seamless access. Signage is in English and Telugu, and station staff are usually helpful. Use it to reach areas like Ameerpet, Parade Ground, HITEC City, and Kukatpally.

TSRTC buses are dirt-cheap (think ₹10–₹30 per ride), but figuring out routes can be tough for first-timers. Bus numbers are displayed on the front, and many buses now have scrolling LED boards in English. You can pay in cash, but keep exact change if possible.

The **MMTS train** system links parts of the old and new city—great for local commuters, not super helpful for most tourists unless you're staying near a station. Schedules are unpredictable and infrastructure is dated.

Auto rickshaw tips: Don't hesitate to walk away if the driver refuses to use the meter or quotes something ridiculous. A good line is, "Meter lagaaiye, bhaiya" ("Please use the meter, brother"). If it still doesn't work, use **Ola Auto**. It's usually cheaper and avoids haggling.

Common scams:

- Drivers quoting 3x the price to foreigners.

- Taking long detours "because of traffic."

- Fake taxi booths outside train stations or airports.

Apps like **RTO Hyderabad** or fare calculators can give you official rate charts if you want a benchmark.

Safety tips:

- Don't travel during rush hours if you can help it—buses and metro coaches get very crowded.

- Keep an eye on your bag and phone.

- Travel light. You don't want to be that person navigating a crowded bus with a roller suitcase.

If you're confident, public transport in Hyderabad can be a cheap and local way to see the city. But for shorter stays, mix it with cabs and metro to save time and energy.

How women can navigate Hyderabad safely and confidently

Hyderabad is generally considered one of India's safer metro cities, but that doesn't mean you should throw caution to the wind. Like anywhere, awareness and a little local know-how go a long way.

Let's talk **dressing smart**. You don't need to be in full traditional gear, but modesty is appreciated, especially in religious or older areas. Think covered shoulders, longer skirts or pants, and nothing too sheer or clingy. In upscale neighborhoods, you'll see plenty of modern fashion—but blending in can make life smoother.

Solo female travelers tend to feel most comfortable staying in areas like **Banjara Hills**, **Jubilee Hills**, or **HITEC City**—they're safe, well-lit, and easy to navigate. Avoid remote or poorly reviewed accommodations, especially those with vague security measures.

The **Hyderabad Metro** has **women-only coaches**—look for the pink signage. It's a calm, respectful space, especially during rush hours.

If you need help, dial **112** (the all-India emergency helpline). There are also **local police patrol units** around tourist spots and metro stations. Most hotel staff will gladly step in to help if something feels off.

Safety apps like **Safetipin**, **bSafe**, or **MySafetipin** are worth downloading. You can also share live locations with friends or hotel staff when using app-based cabs.

Getting unwanted attention? A firm but polite "No, thank you" or simply walking away usually works. Avoid engaging too much with overly curious strangers. Most interactions are harmless, but trust your gut.

Going out at night? Stick to **established venues** in Banjara Hills or HITEC City. Avoid unlit areas and always pre-arrange your ride back. Ask your hotel to call a cab or use ride apps with trip tracking.

Dining solo is common and totally okay—pick cafés or chain restaurants with plenty of foot traffic. For visiting mosques or temples, carry a scarf and follow posted dress codes. Women are usually welcome, but some places have separate entry paths or prayer zones.

Hyderabad is a city that respects women, but being prepared helps you feel confident. Walk like you belong, carry yourself with calm, and don't hesitate to ask for help when needed.

Day trip logistics — getting out of the city and back in one piece

You've soaked in the city. Now you want a breather. Good news—Hyderabad's surroundings offer some solid day trips, but getting the logistics right is key to enjoying them.

Ramoji Film City is the easiest choice. It's about **30 km** from the city and takes 1–1.5 hours by cab. You can book a **package day tour** online (which includes transport and entry), or just take an **Uber** early in the morning. It's huge, so start early and wear comfy shoes.

Nagarjuna Sagar (about 150 km) is beautiful but a stretch for a true day trip. If you're not up for a 6-hour round trip, consider making it an overnight or skipping it. The roads are decent, but not always fast.

Yadagirigutta, a popular temple town about **60 km** away, is doable in a day. You can take a **TSRTC bus**, hire a **private cab**, or join a **temple tour**. Expect crowds on weekends and during festival times.

Bidar (in Karnataka, 140 km away) is historically rich and under the radar. Buses and trains exist, but the easiest way is a private cab with a fixed rate. Be honest with yourself—this is a 5 a.m. departure type of day.

Tips for successful day trips:

- **Leave early** (like before 7 a.m.) to beat traffic.

- **Pack snacks, water, sunscreen**, and a **power bank**.

- Don't assume you'll find great food options at the destination.

- For remote areas, **carry cash**—UPI may not work everywhere.

- **Arrange your return ride in advance**, especially if using a cab. Signal can be weak in some locations.

- Avoid late-night travel back into the city, especially from unfamiliar areas.

For first-timers or families, **guided tours** can be a good bet. They handle logistics, and you won't get stuck figuring out return transport at dusk.

Apps like **MakeMyTrip**, **RedBus**, or **Goibibo** are useful for checking bus and tour options. Or simply ask your hotel concierge—they often have vetted contacts for trusted drivers.

Hyderabad's outskirts have their gems—you just need to plan smarter than Google and pack like a local.

CHAPTER 4: TASTE HYDERABAD — WHAT TO EAT (AND WHAT NOT TO MISS)

Must-try dishes: Biryani (of course), but also what else?

Start with the legend: **Hyderabadi biryani**. Long-grain basmati, layers of tender meat or veggies, fragrant spices—you'll taste history in every bite. It's rich, aromatic, and, yes, a bit indulgent. But don't stop there.

Haleem is the culinary star of **Ramadan**. Slow-cooked wheat, lentils, meat, and ghee—it's creamy comfort in a bowl. Seek it at night markets, especially around **Charminar**.

Kheema samosas—tiny, crisp, and stuffed with spicy minced meat—are perfect for a snack break.

Pathar ka gosht: goat or lamb grilled on a hot stone. Smoky, tender, and best shared over stories.

Double ka meetha (bread pudding with saffron, nuts, and condensed milk) is dessert royalty—sneak in a spoonful, trust me.

Nihari: slow-cooked beef shank stew, often served at dawn. Deep, spicy, and perfect over naan.

Khatti dal: tangy, tamarind-laced lentils that pair beautifully with rice or roti.

Bagara baingan: baby aubergines in a creamy, nutty sauce—rich without the heaviness. A vegetarian must.

Expect: biryani to hit you full-on spice and aroma; haleem to surprise you with its velvety texture; pathar ka gosht with smoky char; and double ka meetha drilling sweetness across your taste buds. Some dishes (nihari, halaal snacks) are heavy—shared plates are better.

Local food joints, hole-in-the-walls, and royal kitchens

Let's go deep.

Beloved local eateries and dhabas:

- **Hotel Shadab**, Old City: classic biryani and haleem; dive in at lunch, avoid lunchtime crowds.

- **Bawarchi**, RTC X Roads: solid biryani, central, reliable.

- **Gokul Chat**, Banjara Hills: for spicy chaats, lip-smacking flavors, and big lines during evenings.

Tiny shops and street stalls:

- **Madina Kachori House** (Chowmahalla area): try kheema samosas at dusk.

- **Nayaab Haleem**, Charminar: Ramadan-only, ultra-authentic.

- **Kababiwala**, Abids: succulent seekh kebabs at lunchtime.

High-end/royal kitchens:

- **Taj Falaknuma's Elephant Bar**: luxurious Biryani with a view—but costly.

- **Palace Restaurant**, Banjara Hills: leather booths, regal ambiance, Hyderabadi classics.

- **Chutneys**, multiple locations: upscale vegetarian South Indian fare.

Heads up: some street stalls don't open before 4 p.m., others close by 8 p.m. Wear comfy shoes. Dhaba vibes can get noisy and crowded—solo diners do well at stalls with shared tables. Families? Dine early. Couples love palace-style spots—book ahead.

Where vegetarians (and vegans) won't feel left out

Hyderabad isn't just meat and spices—it's got a vibrant veggie scene, too.

Breakfast classics: dosas, idlis, vadas, sambar, rasam, poha, upma, and **pulihora** (tamarind rice) are everywhere at tiffin centers.

Local specialties:

- **Gutti vankaya**—stuffed brinjals in rich masala sauce.

- **Aloo kurma**—potatoes in a coconut-and-peanut gravy.

Look for vegetarian-only restaurants like **Pista House** (North Indian thalis), **Chutneys** (South Indian), or small Jain eateries in the Old City.

For vegans, ask about **no curd/ghee** in curries. Words to look for: "veg," "sada" (plain), "curd/khoa/ghee"—use caution if strict.

In food courts or street stalls, point-and-smell smart. Fresh coconut chutney is usually veggie, but sometimes dripping in ghee. Best to ask a local staffer or say "no ghee" politely.

Food safety tips: How to eat well without hugging the toilet

Here's how to enjoy cuisine without compromising health:

Choose stalls with visible crowds—they turn over stock fast.

Stick to **hot, fresh food**. If a dish is sitting out, skip it. That steamed millet dosa? It'll taste better than a soggy salad.

Avoid ice in cold drinks; go with sealed cold drinks or hot chai.

Wash hands before meals—hand sanitizer is your friend. Keep **ORS (rehydration salts)** or **probiotics** handy.

Small stash: bottled water, anti-diarrheal, motion sickness pills, hand wipes.

Kids or older travelers? Let them ease in—no full biryani on day one. Skip overly spicy items until your stomach adjusts.

During festivals, chaos can lead to hygiene slip-ups. Opt for places you trust or eat simpler fare.

It's common to eat street food fearlessly—just be thoughtful. Hybrid strategy: one local stall, one café a day. That usually does the trick.

Sweet tooth satisfaction: Irresistible desserts you'll crave later

Let's wrap up on something sweet.

Qubani ka meetha: slow-cooked apricots with sugar syrup and lightly roasted nuts. Tangy, sweet, unforgettable.

Double ka meetha: Hyderabadi bread pudding—rich and creamy, great with chai.

You'll also find **badam ki jali** (crisp almond wafer), **khubani halwa** (dense apricot fudge), **jalebi** (sticky spirals), and **khova puri** (sweetened fried dough).

Best spots:

- **Karachi Bakery**: iconic for fruit biscuits and plum cakes.

- **Almond House**: wide range of Indian sweets, straddles hygienic and traditional.

- **Chowmahalla Palace** tea area: try desserts with a historic backdrop.

Some sweets travel well as souvenirs (biscuits, dry halwa); others melt in Hyderabad's heat—eat those fresh or buy early in the day.

Dessert pairing tip: silky double ka meetha with strong chai. Or apricot halwa at sunset, leaning back on a bench, letting the sweetness linger.

CHAPTER 5: THE HEART OF HYDERABAD — HISTORY, HERITAGE & ICONIC SITES

Charminar, Chowmahalla, and the Old City's royal pulse

Step into Hyderabad's Old City and you're instantly immersed in sheer energy. Start at the **Charminar**—that unforgettable mosque with four towering minarets. Up close, you'll feel the buzz: vendors shouting, spices hanging in stalls, and the echoes of footsteps on stone. Yes, it's touristy. But it's also real. Visit just after sunrise (around 8 a.m.) to beat the heat and the crowds. Budget 1–1.5 hours—enough to soak it in and climb to the balcony (if you're up for a few flight of steep steps and small crowds).

Next stop: a short walk (or auto ride) to **Chowmahalla Palace**. Think royal courtyards, ornate arches, and vintage cars tucked away inside. It's less crowded, more elegant, a quieter echo of the Nizam era. You can use your Charminar ticket for a small discount—a nice bonus. Budget 1–2 hours here, unless you want to browse every exhibit.

Now, slow down. Wander the warren of lanes around Laad Bazaar. Bangles sparkle overhead, fragrant kebab skewers sizzle in the air, and every now and then a door opens to a quiet shrine. If you feel hot and overwhelmed, duck into a local chai stall—try cutting chai and osmania biscuits. Pause, sip, breathe.

Some tips: Bring cash—many shops won't accept cards. Be wary of any guide who "just wants to show you around." Decline kindly or walk away. Avoid entering courtyards that suddenly charge for a photo-op. Charm means charm, but only pay where signage shows official rates (usually under ₹50–100 per site). Dress modestly, especially inside prayer areas—cover shoulders and knees.

Accessibility note: Charminar's stairs rule out strollers and wheelchairs going up, though ground-level areas are accessible. Chowmahalla Palace has ramps in some sections, but not all—better for those who can walk short distances.

A good afternoon might look like this: Charminar → Chowmahalla → lane-hopping and lunch at a local biryani joint (Hotel Shadab or Bawarchi*. Finish with rooftop chai and a view of the minarets at **Chicha's** or a nearby café.

Golkonda Fort: Echoes, tunnels, legends, and the views

Golkonda isn't just another fort. It's dramatic—the kind of place where you clap at the base and your echo sounds like thunder on the hill. That's the famed acoustic trick designed centuries ago to warn the royals of invaders.

It's built by kings who carved escape tunnels through the rock—literally a castle made for intrigue. Climb to the top and you're rewarded with sweeping old-city vistas. Some stairs are steep, some paths rocky. If you struggle with stamina, take your time or skip a section or two.

Early morning (7 a.m.–9 a.m.) or late afternoon (3 p.m.–5 p.m.) are the best visiting windows: cooler, calmer, and the light is beautiful for photos.

Expect to spend around **2–3 hours** exploring. Tickets are affordable (roughly ₹25–40 local, ₹100–150 foreign), and a small fee gets you a guide who knows all the secrets. Ask about the gate-of-no-return and the way tunnels worked—it's worth it.

There are clean restrooms and small water stalls near the entrance. Bring a bottle, hat, and sunscreen. Skip the clap echo demo if there are crowds—it gets old fast. The **evening sound-and-light show**, held most nights (₹200–300), brings the history alive under floodlights—but only go if you're not exhausted from climbing all day.

Families with kids—take breaks, and maybe bring snacks. Solo travelers might prefer daytime visits when more people are around and areas feel safer. Late evening after the show can leave some secluded paths dimly lit.

Qutb Shahi tombs, Mecca Masjid & beyond

Just a short ride from Chowmahalla, the **Qutb Shahi tombs** feel like a secret garden of grandeur. These domed structures house the remains of Hyderabad's founders, each octagonal marvel surrounded by quiet lawns and architecture that's both ornate and relaxed. Restoration work has cleared away years of overgrowth, but it's still peaceful enough to nearly forget the city bustle. Spend an hour wandering. A guide can add color—who rocket-launched a gold-plated throne into the sky, or why the arches are shaped that way.

From there, head to **Mecca Masjid**, one of India's largest mosques. Built with bricks from Mecca, the scale is breathtaking. Modest dress is required—cover shoulders and legs. Ask to remove your shoes at the designated area, and be respectful—don't talk during prayer. Visit outside prayer times (not during midday on Fridays) and spend 15–20 minutes inside soaking in the stillness. Photography is allowed in the courtyard but steer clear of Wi-Fi hotspots used for prayer.

If you want more history, here are quiet gems nearby:

- **Paigah Tombs** are tucked behind a mosque, with intricate carvings and far fewer tourists—best for architecture lovers.

- **Toli Masjid**, a small but graceful 17th-century mosque north of Charminar. Great for focused photos or calm.

Walking distance between these is 1–2 km, but autos are easy to find. You can bundle them into an afternoon—tomb complex first, then mosque, then tea break at a local stall. Skip the mosque tour if you're pressed for time and let the tombs and Charminar hold the day.

Museums that don't feel boring

If you only have one museum day, make it count at the **Salar Jung Museum**. It's massive—sometimes overwhelming. But focus on a few things: the miniature painting gallery, the European decorative arts wing, and that iconic reclining Buddha. Use a museum map. Spend 2–3 hours max, then take a chai break if you feel burned out. Entry is affordable (₹20 for locals, ₹200 for foreigners—2025 rates).

Nearby, the **Nizam's Museum** inside Purani Haveli is a compact peek at royal life—luxury carriages, jeweled wardrobes, vintage photos. Friendly guides sometimes hang around to explain tidbits like how the Nizams paid staff not in rupees, but in uncut pearls.

If you like archaeology or ancient art, the **Telangana State Archaeology Museum** near Public Gardens isn't huge, but has interesting Buddhist statues and stone sculptures. It's low-key, quick, and pleasant—plan an hour.

Many travelers skip the overhyped "Science Museum" or galleries with dated exhibits—they're often poorly maintained or pricey. No shame in skipping them.

All museums have locker facilities, signs in English, and basic restrooms. Cameras are usually allowed but no flash—check signage by the entrance. If you're traveling with kids, the Salar Jung has carved chests and colorful textiles that keep them entertained—even if they can't read every caption.

Walking tours and why they beat tour buses every time

You could ride past Charminar in an air-conditioned bus—and miss almost everything. Walking, though? You'll hear hawkers shouting, smell spices roasting, notice a hidden shrine behind a wall, or peek into a household shrine off an alley. You'll feel the city's pulse.

Groups start small—6 to 12 people—and usually cost ₹500–1,500 per person for 2–3 hours. Try operators like **Telangana Tourism** or boutique groups led by heritage lovers (search "Hyderabad heritage walk"). You can pick a theme: food-focused, architecture, photography, or mix it up.

These tours run early morning or late afternoon—perfect to escape midday heat. Bring comfy shoes, water, and a basic understanding of the route. Evenings are charming, but smaller groups feel safer then.

Walking beats bus tours because it gives you human-scale stories, not slogans. Bus tours are fine if mobility is an issue, but don't expect local color—they take you past sites without letting you pause. On foot, if you spot an interesting spice shop, you can duck in for a taste.

Booking is easy—check sites like **Viator**, **GetYourGuide**, or ask your hotel concierge. A good guide will know shortcuts, hidden cafés, and bathrooms—something a bus driver won't tell you.

For travellers seeking real texture, walking in the Old City beats staring out a tinted window any day.

CHAPTER 6: CULTURE, RELIGION, AND DAILY Life — WHAT MAKES HYDERABAD FEEL LIKE HYDERABAD

Language, dress codes, and street etiquette

Hyderabad hums in four languages: **Telugu**, **Urdu**, **Hindi**, and **English**. Outdoors, in markets and local neighborhoods, Telugu signs and phrases are everywhere. Urdu pops up around the Old City—especially near Charminar—on shop signs or heard in casual greetings. Hindi is common, especially in shops with tourists. In most tourist-friendly areas, English works just fine.

A few phrases go a long way:

- *"Dhanyavaad/Shukriya"* (thanks)

- *"Salaam alaikum"* (common greeting in Urdu-speaking zones)

- *"Kitna hua?"* (How much?)

  Using them shows you cared enough to learn—and locals appreciate it.

Dress-wise, Hyderabadis balance modern ease with modesty. In business districts, you'll see everything from jeans and tees to kurta-pyjamas. In markets or religious areas, both locals and travelers cover shoulders and legs. Women often wear light shawls or dupattas. Men wear trousers or jeans with short-sleeve shirts. In mosques or temples, cover shoulders, avoid tight clothing.

Street etiquette? Yes, you can haggle—but softly. Think of it like friendly banter, not a negotiation tournament. Always start with a smile. Stand in line—but don't be surprised if it turns into a loose queue where politeness takes over. When crossing, follow locals. Never expect a zebra crossing to save you—ever.

Gestures matter. A thumbs-up is fine. Avoid pointing—use your whole hand instead. If you greet, a quick namaste with palms together (even lip-less) shows respect.

Women in public are comfortable—especially in modern zones. Still, honesty and confidence go a long way. Lock your eyes on your goal, walk with purpose, and you'll mostly glide right past noise.

A Hindu-Muslim cultural blend you won't find anywhere else

Here's the beauty: in Hyderabad, Ramadan iftar dinners sit side by side with Diwali fireworks on the same street. That's not scheduled multiculturalism—it's everyday life.

In some neighborhoods, you'll smell haleem cooking at night and sweet meetha poori from the bakery across the road. During Bonalu, Hindu prayers will follow Islamic chants in the same area. Families—Muslim and Hindu—run the same eateries. Traditions cross boundaries.

Look for this in a single street market: bangles from Hindu artisans, stalls selling rose sharbat for iftar, and Muslim tailors stitching bridal wear. That blend didn't happen overnight—it grew from centuries of coexistence.

To enjoy it respectfully: attend a Muharram procession one day, and the next peek at Ganesh idols being immersed. Ask questions like "What does that ceremony mean for you?" and listen. Be curious, not invasive.

If you join a street feast or are invited into a home for chai during Ramzan or Diwali, a modest gift—like sweets or fruit—is appreciated and always accepted with warmth.

Religion & rituals: What to know when visiting mosques and temples

You're heading into sacred space—here's how to do it right.

Mosques (like Mecca Masjid): remove shoes outside the entrance. Cover shoulders and legs. Women may need a scarf—carry one in your bag. Avoid visiting during Friday prayers (midday). Walk quietly, keep your phone on silent, and stick to the designated visitor areas. Yes, architecture is beautiful. Yes, feel free to admire it—but don't talk loudly or disturb worshippers.

Temples: shoes come off. Sometimes socks too—watch what locals do. Men and women may enter through different gates. Hands folded (sometimes called "Namaste") shows respect. If you see priests performing rituals, step back quietly. You can offer a small donation or light a candle if donations boxes are visible.

In both places: look for signs marking "No photography." If in doubt, just ask softly, "May I take a photo?" Most people smile and say yes—if they don't, no need to push.

Peak times like Friday afternoons in mosques or Saturdays in temples can be crowded. Visit right after morning calls or mid-afternoon for a calmer experience.

Local celebrations, weddings, and what that loud street procession really is

In Hyderabad, celebrations aren't behind gates—they're on the street. And they come in waves.

Wedding baraats arrive with upbeat music and dancing uncles holding flags—look like revelers, and they may smile and wave for a picture. You're watching happiness unfold—and yes, cameras are usually okay. Just ask first if you want a photo close up.

Ganesh Chaturthi comes with colorful fun—large Ganesha idols on trucks roll through neighborhoods with drumbeats that pulsate for hours. Stand back to avoid the flood, but don't be shy about being part of the atmosphere.

During **Ramzan**, evening bazaars glow with lights and food stalls. Join with respect: queue politely, use both hands to receive food from vendors, and pause before eating in public out of respect for fasting locals.

Muharram processions (especially in the Old City) are solemn—black clothes, chants, heartfelt ritual. Stand quietly at the edge, observe in stillness, reflect. Photos? Better to skip.

Bonalu and **Bathukamma** blend devotion and festivity. If people welcome you, it's okay to join briefly. But if you feel unsure, smile, step back, and soak it in. No need to mingle unless it feels natural.

Know this: celebrations may close bazaars early or create loud pockets late into the night. If you're staying nearby, earplugs can be a godsend.

How to respectfully blend in (and when to just be a curious tourist)

There's a sweet balance in Hyderabad between blending in and standing out—both are okay.

On one hand, do simple gestures: hold your "thank you" with a slight head bob, remove your shoes before stepping into prayer spaces, fold hands as locals do. These small actions matter.

But you're not a local—and that's okay, too. If you speak with enthusiasm, ask "What is that?" and accept answers with a smile, you'll get more invitations than you'd expect.

If someone invites you to join a ritual, feel free to—if it feels comfortable. But avoid jumping in mid-ceremony. Wait for an opening cue or ask, "Is it okay to...?"

Locals understand you're not local. Effort, even imperfect, counts. A head covering that's slightly off-center is fine. A shy "Hello" in Urdu is charming. Humility is your friend.

Big takeaway: An unforced smile and authentic curiosity matter more than flawless cultural knowledge. Be present. Listen. Learn. And know that Hyderabad will welcome you—not because you're perfect, but because you've shown respect.

CHAPTER 7: SHOPPING & MARKETS — WHAT TO BUY AND WHERE TO BARGAIN

Laad Bazaar, pearls, perfumes, bangles and bling

Walk into **Laad Bazaar** and your senses go into overdrive. Glittering glass bangles tower overhead, attar perfumes whisper from hidden stalls, and scooters weave through the crowds like busy bees. This place is sensory chaos—but it's also treasure-laden.

Here's how to get through the noise and find the gems. First, visit between **10 a.m. and 1 p.m.**, or after **4 p.m.**—avoid midday crush and scorching sun. Trust your instincts: stalls with neat displays and friendly vendors tend to be more reliable than the frantic, shouting ones.

Pearls are Hyderabad's pride. Look for stalls that let you inspect each string under natural light. Real, freshwater pearls will feel cool to the touch and have slight variations. Expect to pay ₹2,000–5,000 (medium quality) or ₹10,000+ for fine strands. Aim for shops near the main bazaar entrance—Hyderabadi Pearls & Jewels is a local favorite with better reputation than random carts deeper inside.

Bangles come in lacquered wood, glass, metal, or lac. If one rattles like plastic, skip it. Pick sturdy glass bangles—even if they cost more, they last longer. Try **Saeed Bangles** near Charminar—stacked with colors and styles, they cater to both bridal hunting and casual bling.

If perfume catches your interest, stop at **Zarqa's Attar** just off the bazaar's main lane. It's mixed on-site; you can try tiny samples. To avoid headache, start with milder scents like oud or rose, and test on paper before skin. Avoid pre-bottled attars with glitter around the neck—they're cheaper and often diluted.

Women may get extra attention—and not always welcome. Smile and say "No, thank you" firmly if someone pushes. Men shopping are often given more space. Solo shoppers in the Old City can feel overwhelmed, so bring a companion or keep your phone out—just that small awareness helps.

Budget 2–3 hours here if you hope to browse, haggle, taste street snacks, and snap a few photos. Keep valuables close—Laad Bazaar is crowded, and scarves or light jackets with hidden pockets help. And if it feels like sensory overload? That's normal. Step aside into a side alley, get a cold drink, breathe, and get back in.

Modern malls vs. old markets — where the magic really is

Hyderabad's malls—**GVK One**, **Inorbit**, **Sarath City Capital**—are clean, sleek, and full of international brands, polished restrooms, food courts, and air-conditioning. Great for a day out with family, quiet shopping, kids, or catching a movie.

But the real magic? That lives in the old streets.

Sultan Bazaar sells textiles, electronics, and household goods. **Moazzam Jahi Market** is the place for fruit, local snacks, and jaggery. **Begum Bazaar** is a chaotic wholesale hub—fresh spices, metalware, kitchen tools. These markets are colorful, noisy, and bursting with character.

If you're short on time, combine both: spend a morning in Laad Bazaar or Moazzam Jahi, then cool off in a mall in the afternoon. Malls open by **10 a.m.**, markets happen best before **1 p.m.** Malls also have better parking and calmer vibes—good for solo women or older travelers. Markets offer nostalgia, personality—and bargains—but require patience and a good sense for rhythm.

What's worth your money (and what's just tourist bait)

Hyderabad has real treasures and overblown gimmicks. Here's the cheat sheet:

Worth it:

- **Pearl necklaces** with proper quality checks—lasting and beautiful.

- **Hand-mixed attar** perfumes—light, long-lasting, and unique to the region.

- **Lacquered or glass bangles**—authentic, stylish, and culturally rooted.

- **Kalamkari fabrics**—hand-printed cloths that hold up and tell stories.

Tourist bait to skip:

- Cheapo trinket "pearls" sold for ₹50–100—they're plastic-coated beads.

- Mass-produced "Hyderabad" T-shirts—generic, everywhere, forgettable.

- Perfumes bottled in plastic containers with no authenticity stamps.

Price ranges to keep in mind:

- Pearls: ₹2,000–5,000 for modest strands, ₹10,000+ for premium.

- Attars: ₹200–500 per 10 ml bottle—sample high-end ones for more.

- Bangles: ₹200–1,000 a dozen depending on quality and material.

Ask locals or your hotel for trusted shops—not random stalls. Backpackers should focus on small affordable tokens; couples might invest in a fine bangle set or pearl piece;

families could bring home spices or fabric rather than heavy jewelry.

Polite "no thank you" goes a long way to exit an overly aggressive stall. If the deal seems too good to be true, it probably is.

Bargaining tips that won't make you feel awkward

Yes, you *should* haggle in markets—but it doesn't have to be awkward or confrontational. Think of bargaining as a dance, not a duel.

Here's a friendly approach:

- Start by asking "Kitna?" (How much?)

- Let them give a high price.

- Counter with **50–60%** of that—and smile.

  o "₹400?" instead of "₹1,000?"

- They might laugh, hold firm. Offer 10–20% more than your ask, and close with "Theek hai?" (Okay?)

- If it still feels high, say "No, thanks" and walk away. They might call you back with a better offer.

Keep notes small. Carry ₹500s or ₹200s—not ₹2,000s flapping in your hand.

If you're a solo female shopper, bargaining in front of your group (or a friend) can feel easier than on your own. Older travelers often fare better when someone else is with them.

Remember—stay polite and smile. If the vendor is friendly, chuckle, and let the price settle. Flowers at the end of the interaction is best—thank them, say goodbye.

How to ship stuff home if your suitcase gives up

Bought more than planned? There are options.

India Post at the GPO is reliable and cheap. You'll need to fill out basic customs forms, pay by weight, and expect **1–3**

weeks delivery to most countries. Packaging can be minimal unless you ask for a box.

FedEx/DHL counters at malls or outside Old City offer faster service (3–5 days) and better insurance—but costlier. Expect to pay ₹3,000–7,000 for a 5 kg package abroad.

Local couriers near Charminar offer a middle ground—ask around your hotel or shop for a buttoned-up agent. Delivery generally takes **7–10 days**.

Packaging tips:

- Let the shop wrap fragile items—they know how. For fabric: roll gently to reduce damage.

- Get a weight estimate before committing. Rule: if shipping costs nearly equal the item value, bring your own suitcase.

Sorting:

- **India Post** = slow, affordable, minimal packaging.

- **International courier** = fast, insulated, more paperwork.

- **Local agent** = middle path in price and speed.

Keep receipts, tracking numbers, and customs forms organized in a folder. And yeah—sometimes buying a second cheap suitcase and checking it is smarter than shipping delicate glass bangles.

CHAPTER 8: OFFBEAT HYDERABAD — HIDDEN GEMS YOU'D NEVER FIND ON GOOGLE

Stepwells, secret cafés, lakeside spots and rooftop views

You've seen the monuments. Now let's wander off the beaten path.

Imagine slipping into a narrow alley tucked between modern shops—and suddenly stepping into the quiet cool of **Badi Baoli**, an ancient stepwell hemmed in by concrete walls. It's a hidden pocket of serenity, where the stones underfoot whisper of centuries past. Visit in the late afternoon, when the sun hits just right, and you'll often have it to yourself. Solo travelers will feel calm here; the vibe is respectful, hushed.

Then there's the handful of **secret cafés**—tiny places with three tables, handwritten menus, and zero Wi-Fi. One such gem in Jubilee Hills has the best cold brew you'll find for miles. Learn it by word-of-mouth—ask your guesthouse host or a friendly barista. Show up mid-morning, settle into a wooden chair, order that single-origin coffee, and open your notebook. Bliss.

Looking for a pause by water? Head to one of those overlooked benches beside a neighborhood **lakeside park**—try a small pond near Manikonda or one tucked behind local housing blocks. You'll hear nothing but birds, ripples, and distant scooter hums. It's the kind of spot where Hyderabad's noise softens and the cityscape seems kinder.

At sunset, hunt down a **rooftop viewpoint**—not the fancy hotel kind, but a lifted terrace with mismatched chairs and tea served in chipped cups. On a clear day, you'll see both old city domes and the distant shimmer of Hitech City towers. Go early, buy chai from a nearby stall, and let that moment land.

The art scene, indie bookstores, and quiet escapes

Hyderabad's quieter creative corners are where you breathe differently.

Head to **Kalakriti Art Gallery** for intimate local exhibitions. It's rarely crowded and often free. Settle yourself on a bench, watch visitors meander, and take five minutes to linger at one piece before moving on.

Nearby, **Lamakaan** has a courtyard that feels like an indie dream—open-mic, poetry nights, a sense of casual community. It's casual: drop in mid-afternoon, sip a bookshop espresso, and you might catch someone rehearsing a folk tune. Solo travelers will find it welcoming. Bring a journal.

Craving silence and books? Try a tucked-away **library or bookstore** in Basheerbagh—one with more cats than customers. Ask the staff for obscure poetry or regional chapters in translation. They'll smile, recommend, and perhaps brew you chai.

These spots are for the quiet traveler—someone who'd rather sketch than Instagram. Tip: check opening times online and always get a second chai if you linger.

Places even locals forget about

These are the places your taxi driver might not know, but your walking guide will.

There's a **colonial clock tower** behind a government office in Secunderabad that ticks like a soft heartbeat—only if you wander past the official gates. Or an unused **railway quarter** near Falaknuma, with broken tracks and painted walls peeling in pastels. Spooky, peaceful, and totally photo-worthy.

Some mosques have forgotten **stepwells in their courtyards**, overhung by vines—stumble in behind seldom-used doors. They feel eerie in the afternoon hush. Most are safe, but solo visitors should tread respectfully and avoid after dark.

Quiet cemeteries, too—old Christian or Muslim graveyards shaded by banyan trees, names in English and Urdu fading. They call to travelers who care about layers, silence, and old stories.

These places aren't made for tourists. Go slow, take notes, make eye contact if someone inside notices you. Avoid loud photography or disruptive behavior. Trust your instinct, and bring a friend if it feels off at all.

Underrated temples, old havelis, and colonial corners

Beyond the big temples lie a few you won't find on signs.

Keesaragutta Temple sits on a small hill outside town—modest, peaceful, with ancient stone pillars embossed with gods. The climb is gentle, the payoff is quiet devotion and sunrise views.

Closer in, there are **hidden Jain shrines** behind apartment buildings—almost invisible unless a neighbor points them out. Their marble idols and prayer bells are calming, unassuming.

Old **havelis**, crumbling in narrow lanes, offer a glimpse of faded splendor—wooden balconies, carved doors, and cats weaving in and out. Some are still lived in. Walk past respectfully; peek, notice, but avoid disrupting anyone's space.

Colonial relics like a **vintage clocktower, a forgotten post office**, or a small **Anglo-Indian bungalow** in Jubilee Hills are tucked behind newer buildings. They're charming but often unnoticed—go look, sketch a window, and feel how the city grew around it.

These are for travelers focused on emotional texture—not selfies. Bring anything that lets you collect those moments: a sketchpad, a voice memo, an old-school camera. And yes—locals who still live near these spots often have great stories if you pause and listen.

Day trips that don't feel touristy

When you're ready to escape the city, these are solid low-tourist options:

Medak Fort and Cathedral: About 90 km away, with Gothic arches inside Medak Cathedral just east of the fort. Take a daytime train or rent a cab early—drive is safe, roads are decent, and the view from the ramparts is clean and calm. Spend time in the church where local priests are often happy to chat.

Pocharam Lake: Less manicured than bigger parks, with pebble beaches, fishing families, and wood-fired tea stalls. Bring snacks and binoculars—look for migratory birds in winter. A weekend morning there feels like a rural reset.

Bhongir Fort: A 50 km climb up a round hilltop—not strenuous, but uplifting. Pack a picnic, enjoy the breeze, and count the city lights below. Go early to avoid afternoon heat; bring water.

Take these trips on weekdays if possible—Saturdays are local outdoors day and can get busier. Public buses reach Medak and Bhongir—but renting a cab is easier and worth it. Pack snacks, sunscreen, charger, and enjoy road songs while you go.

These day trips aren't hype—they're quiet moments of extra space. You'll still cross paths with locals, but in a good way—not crowded buses, not rushed tours. Just real, low-key exploration.

CHAPTER 9: MODERN HYDERABAD — TECH CITY VIBES AND WHAT'S CHANGED

Hitech City, start-up buzz, and the new Hyderabad

Hyderabad has grown fast—and you'll see that most clearly in **Hitech City**, where glass towers and tech campuses mark the skyline. This isn't just outsourced call centers or software support; it's big names like Microsoft, Google, Amazon—and dozens of hungry startups in co-working spaces and innovation hubs. The vibe here is energized and aspirational, full of caffeinated ambition and shared Wi-Fi.

For the traveler, it means a few practical perks: great cafés, coworking lounges with day passes, and slick malls like Forum Sujana. But you'll also notice traffic has changed—roads are busier in office hours, and more ride-share cars zip by. If you walk those tree-lined streets, you'll overhear conversations about pitch decks and blockchain, or catch yoga groups stretching between meetings.

If you're a **digital nomad or business traveler**, Hitech is worth a peek. Grab coffee at BlueTokai, check out a co-working space like **T-Hub**, and ask around for evening startup meetups. For others? It's a contrast worth seeing—especially after wandering the Old City earlier. It shows Hyderabad isn't just historic; it's reinventing itself, and fast.

Where young locals hang out — cafés, clubs, and creative spaces

Looking to feel the pulse of Hyderabad's creative youth? Try brunching at **Odeon Social** or **The Gallery Café**—both blend artsy vibes with solid espresso and open seating for laptop dwellers. Weekends come alive with open-mic poetry nights at Lamakaan, or loft-style gatherings at Phoenix Arena.

At night, **Heart Cup Coffee** and **Hylife Brewing Company** in Jubilee Hills host jazz nights or stand-up. These places feel inclusive—LGBTQ+ posters visible, diverse crowds, and staff who won't blink if a solo stranger shows up late. Ideal for couples or solo women looking for safe, fun scenes. Just know cover charges or happy hours vary—ask ahead.

Expect polished feels, musical chatter, and casual price tags. If everything feels too curated, head deeper into local neighborhoods—teahouses around Gachibowli stay open late and feel more homegrown.

Health & wellness: Gyms, yoga, and where to detox after food marathons

Need balance after all that biryani? Hit a **one-day access gym** like **Gold's Gym** or **Cult.fit**—they're plentiful in Banjara and Jubilee Hills, and day passes cost about ₹300–500.

Morning yogis prefer **Public Gardens** or **Hitech City Park**—open-air sessions start at sunrise, often for donations. Look for mats laid in quiet corners under banyan trees.

For a treat-win over your gut: **Wellness cafés** serving smoothie bowls and nut milks have popped up—try **Chicory** or **The Health Factory**. Need pampering? Head to **AyurVAID** spa or **O2 Spa**—part of major hotels—for relaxing Ayurvedic massages (₹1,500–2,500).

Jogging? Try **Hussain Sagar lakefront** at dawn—often smooth, scenic, and well-lit. Expect locals walking dogs and feeding pigeons. At night it's quieter but still safe.

Digital nomad friendly? (Spoiler: Yes — if you know where to go)

Hyderabad is growing into a hidden gem for nomads. Here's what makes it decent—if you're smart:

Wi-Fi & coworking: JioFiber and Airtel broadband cover major neighborhoods well. **Co-working spots** like T-Hub (near Gachibowli), **Workburg** (Kondapur), and **91Springboard** (Hitech City) offer day passes of ₹500–800/day and reliable internet.

Cafés that let you stay: Horn OK Please, Brew Room, and Roastery Coffee House tend to welcome laptop stays—just buy a drink or two per hour.

Neighborhoods: Hitech, Jubilee, and Banjara offer cafes, gyms, parks, and coworking—all walkable. Internet backup with data SIM is handy for power outages or backup.

Challenges: midday AC outages can sneak up on you, so pack a power bank. Traffic can delay meetings, so locate near your coworking space. Dress codes are casual-smart: jeans and kurtas work, shorts less so.

Nomad communities connect via **Facebook groups** ("Digital Nomads Hyderabad") or local Meetup panels. Online, you'll find casual meetups and recommendations daily.

Hyderabad after dark — is it safe, fun, or both?

Let's talk nightlife—and safety—plainly.

After **8 p.m.**, the city comes alive. Rooftop bars in Jubilee Hills glow with fairy lights and chatter, live music punches at Heart Cup Coffee, and chai shops around Hussain Sagar bustle with late-night snacks. Restaurant areas in Hitech are lit until 11 p.m. or midnight.

Safety? Hyderabad is generally calm. **Ola and Uber** are reliable after dark—show driver details to your hotel or share trip status with a friend. Solo women travel fine, though staying in well-lit areas like Jubilee or HITEC City is wise. Avoid wandering in dim Old City lanes past 10 p.m.

The city has no curfew, and local police maintain visible patrols in nightlife zones. If you ever feel uneasy, head to the nearest crowd or ride-share pick-up point.

In short: you can absolutely enjoy Hyderabad after dark. Just choose curated venues or busy lanes, plan your transport ahead, and trust your instincts. Evening rides are usually safe, and the city's relaxed vibe at night is worth pacing slowly through.

CHAPTER 10: SAMPLE ITINERARIES & TRAVEL SMARTS

1-Day, 3-Day, and 5-Day itineraries that don't feel rushed

1-Day Sample
Solo/Couples:

- **7 a.m.:** Sunrise walk and chai by Hussain Sagar lake.

- **8 a.m.:** Hitech City quick metro ride to Ameerpet for auto to Charminar.

- **9 a.m.–11 a.m.:** Explore Charminar + Laad Bazaar (peak before midday heat).

- **11 a.m.:** Short walk to Chowmahalla Palace for cool interiors and history.

- **12:30 p.m.:** Lunch at Hotel Shadab—biryani to beat hunger.

- **2 p.m.:** Taxi to Salar Jung Museum, gentle stroll and gallery stops—wrap by 4 p.m.

- **4:30 p.m.:** Rooftop chai near Charminar.

- **6 p.m.:** Metro to Jubilee Hills for dinner at a café lounge.

- **8 p.m.:** Rooftop bar or relaxed evening walk by the lake.

Families/Older Travelers:

Skip Laad chaos, head to the safer Salar Jung Museum midday. Use cab or wheelchair support.

3-Day Sample

Day 1: Old City loop (as above) with extra time for Qutb Shahi Tombs via afternoon taxi.

Day 2: Early Golkonda Fort visit, lunch in Gachibowli, afternoon in HITEC City & café stop, evening in modern districts.

Day 3: Off-beaten day trip (Pocharam or Medak), soothe the next morning with yoga or slow start by the lake.

5-Day Sample
Days 1–3: As 3-day trip.

Day 4: Explore hidden cafes, libraries, secular strolls through lanes and colonial zones.

Day 5: Shopping + spa day + evening stroll in modern cafés or creative hubs.

In each, build in 30–45 min breaks between sites. Adjust for weather—summer means afternoons rest; winter afternoons are ideal for walks or lakeside time.

What to do if it rains (or your plan goes sideways)

Unexpected rain? Here's your backup plan:

- **Museums:** Engage fully at Salar Jung or Nizam's Museum.

- **Malls:** Inorbit or GVK One for shopping, food, movies.

- **Cafés or bookstores:** Find cozy corners with good coffee and Wi-Fi.

- **Cooking class or spice market visit under shelter.**

- **Major tip:** Keep a compact umbrella and waterproof shoes in your bag.

- Treat it like an unexpected pause—chat with locals, try street food stalls under awnings, or journal in a café. Travel doesn't end when the ceiling leaks; it gets interesting.

How to slow down and travel well

Hyderabad's soul is revealed in pauses:

- Chatting with an auto driver about his neighborhood.

- Sipping chai by a lakeside bench.

- Sketching a bangle stall in Laad Bazaar.

- Browsing dusty shelves in an old library.

Build unplanned moments into your day—30-minute gaps are golden. If you're overwhelmed, skip one big site in favor of wandering on foot. Remember: slow isn't lazy—it's noticing. That's where memories live.

What locals wish tourists knew

- **Dress respectfully** in Old City and religious areas—shoulders and knees covered.

- **Don't assume everyone eats meat**—many locals are vegetarian or follow religious diets.

- **Ask before photographing people**; strangers aren't props.

- **Queue kindly at bus stops or stores**; pushing in feels rude.

- **Smile first**—it's the shortcut to warmth here.

- **Roughly one local tip on forums:** "We appreciate when guests say thank you in Telugu or Urdu—it shows you tried."

Be the traveler you'd want as a guest—aware, considerate, friendly.

Final packing checklist (with zero fluff)

Essentials:

- Cotton clothes + one modest scarf/shawl

- Compact umbrella

- Rehydration salts + basic meds (anti-diarrheal, painkiller)

- Extra phone charger or power bank

- Dual plug adapter (India uses types C/D/M)

- Passport copies + travel insurance info

- Small pouch for cash/cards (anti-theft)

Nice-to-haves:

- Binoculars for lakeside birdwatching

- Light journal/sketchbook + pen

- Reusable water bottle

- Travel clothesline + laundry soap (for slow travel style)

Optional:

- Light yoga mat or foldable travel mat

- Snacks from home (protein bars, nuts, trail mix)

Skip bulky shoes, full-size toiletries, or guidebooks—you'll find food and essentials everywhere.

Parting tips to leave with memories, not regrets

- Book major transport early (flights, trains, Golkonda tickets).

- Pack meds before symptoms arrive—hyderabad's pharmacy is good, but you're in travel mode.

- Accept that traffic is *always* slower than Google says.

- Learn one phrase and use it often—it changes conversations.

- Stop before you're done—save some energy for future nostalgia.

- Ask someone "Where do *you* go on weekends?" and explore that next time.

Take your time. Let Hyderabad surprise you. Say thank you in Telugu, and leave a bit of your heartbeat in the city itself.

Printed in Dunstable, United Kingdom

65513571R00060